Finding information in stories and artifacts brings the past to life.

SCHOLASTIC

LITERACY
PLACE®

Copyright acknowledgments and credits appear on page 128, which constitutes an extension of this copyright page.

Copyright © 1996 by Scholastic Inc.   All rights reserved.   Printed in the U.S.A.
                                             ISBN 0-590-49121-0
                    5 6 7 8 9 10   24   02 01 00 99 98 97

Dig into
an Archaeological Site

Finding information in stories and artifacts brings the past to life.

Meet the Time Detectives

Archaeologists uncover clues to the past.

ARMOR OF
GEORGE CLIFFORD,
THIRD EARL OF
CUMBERLAND

Blued steel decorated with gold
designs
Made in Greenwich, England,
sometime between 1580 and
1585
Height: 69 1 inches

The third earl of Cumberland
wore this armor when he
attended tournaments. At the
tournaments, knights showed
off their skills. This fancy armor
was made for him at the
armor shops in
When th

Look at the Clues

Stories and artifacts provide clues to the past.

Add Up the Evidence

We can piece together a picture of the past by adding up the evidence.

Trade Books

**The following
books accompany this
Time Detectives
SourceBook.**

Biography

AWARD WINNING

**Frederick
Douglass
Fights for
Freedom**

Author

by Margaret
Davidson

Realistic Fiction

AWARD WINNING

**George
Washington's
Breakfast**

Author/
Illustrator

by Jean Fritz
illustrated by
Paul Galdone

Informational Fiction

AWARD WINNING

**Let's Go
Traveling**

Author

by Robin
Rector
Krupp

Historical Fiction

AWARD WINNING

Three Names

Book

by Patricia
MacLachlan
illustrated by
Alexander
Pertzoff

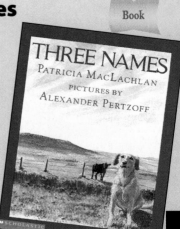

Archaeologists uncover clues to the past.

Meet the Time Detectives

Read a story about a girl who imagines a family's past. Then join real-life kids as they uncover their community's history.

Dig up evidence with archaeologist Ruben Mendoza.

Dive into a treasure hunt—underwater.

WORKSHOP 1

Describe a present-day artifact for time detectives of the future.

ARMOR OF GEORGE CLIFFORD, THIRD EARL OF CUMBERLAND

Blued steel decorated with gold designs
Made in Greenwich, England, sometime between 1580 and 1585
Height: 69½ inches

The third Earl of Cumberland wore this armor when he attended tournaments. At the tournaments, knights showed off their skills. This fancy armor was made for him at the royal armor shops in Greenwich. When the Earl dressed in his armor, he had to put on fourteen

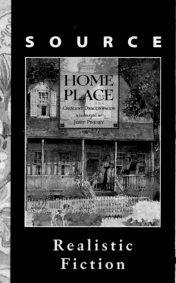
HOME PLACE

BY CRESCENT DRAGONWAGON
ILLUSTRATED BY JERRY PINKNEY

AWARD
WINNING

Book

Every year,
these daffodils come up.
There is no house near them.
There is nobody to water them.
Unless someone happens to come this way,
like us, this Sunday afternoon, just walking,
there is not even anyone to see them.
But still they come up, these daffodils
in a row, a yellow splash
brighter than sunlight, or lamplight, or butter,
in the green and shadow of the woods.
Still they come up, these daffodils,
cups lifted to trumpet
the good news
of spring,

though maybe no one hears
except the wind
and the raccoons who rustle at night
and the deer who nibble delicately
at the new green growth
and the squirrels who jump
from branch to branch
of the old black walnut tree.

But once,
someone lived here.
How can you tell?
Look. A chimney, made of stone,
back there, half-standing yet, though honeysuckle's
grown around it—there must
have been a house here. Look.
Push aside these weeds—here's
a stone foundation, laid on earth.
The house once here was built on it.

And if there was a house, there was
a family.
Dig in the dirt, scratch deep, and what
do you find?
A round blue glass marble, a nail.
A horseshoe and a piece
of plate. A small yellow bottle. A china doll's arm.

Listen. Can you listen, back, far back?
No, not the wind, that's now. But listen,
back, and hear:
  a man's voice, scratchy-sweet, singing "Amazing Grace,"
  a rocking chair squeaking, creaking on a porch,
  the bubbling hot fat in a black skillet, the chicken frying,
  and "Tommy! Get in here this minute! If I have to call you
  one more time—!"
  and "Ah, me, it's hot," and "Reckon it'll storm?"
 "I don't know, I sure hope, we sure could use it,"
  and "Supper! Supper tiiiiime!"

If you look, you can almost see them:
the boy at dusk, scratching in the dirt with his stick, the
uneven swing hanging vacant
in the black walnut tree, listless in the heat;
the girl, upstairs, combing out her long, long hair, unpinning,
unbraiding, and combing, by an oval mirror;
downstairs, Papa washing dishes as Mama sweeps the floor
and Uncle Ferd, Mama's brother, coming in, whistling, back
from shutting up the chickens
for the night, wiping the sweat
from his forehead.
"Ah, Lord, it's hot, even late as it is,"
"Yes, it surely is."
Someone swats
at a mosquito.
Bedtime.

But in that far-back summer night,
the swing begins to sway
as the wind comes up
as the rain comes down
there's thunder there's lightning (that's just like now)
the dry dusty earth soaks up the water
the roots of the plants, like the daffodil bulbs
the mama planted, hidden under the earth, but alive
and growing, the roots
drink it up. A small green snake
coils happily in the wet woods,
and Tommy sleeps straight through the storm. Anne, the girl, who
wishes for a yellow hair ribbon, wakes and then returns to
sleep, like Uncle Ferd, sighing as he dreams
of walking down a long road with change in his pocket. But
the mother wakes, and wakes the father, her husband,
and they sit on the side of the bed,
and watch the rain together,
without saying a word, in the house where everyone else
still sleeps. Her head on Papa's shoulder,
her long hair falling down her back, she's wearing
a white nightgown
that makes her look
almost like a ghost when the lightning flashes.

And now, she *is* a ghost, and we
can only see her
if we try. We're not sure
if we're making her up, or if
we really can see her, imagining
the home place as it might have been, or was, before
the house burned down, or everyone moved away
and the woods moved in.

Her son and daughter, grown and gone, her brother
who went to Chicago, her husband, even
her grandchildren, even her house,
all gone, almost as gone as if
they had never laughed and eaten chicken and rocked,
played and fought and made up,
combed hair and washed dishes and swept,
sang and scratched at mosquito bites.
Almost as gone, but
not quite. Not quite.
They were here.
This was their home.

For each year, in a quiet green place,
where there's only a honeysuckle-vined chimney
to tell you there was ever a house
(if, that is, you happen to travel that way,
and wonder, like we did);
where there's only a marble, a nail, a horseshoe, a piece
of plate, a piece of doll,
a single rotted almost-gone piece of rope swaying
on a black walnut tree limb,
to tell you there was ever a family here;
only deer and raccoons and squirrels
instead of people
to tell you there were living creatures;
each year, still,
whether anyone sees, or not,
whether anyone listens, or not,
the daffodils come up,
to trumpet their good news
forever and forever.

SOURCE

OWL
Magazine

AWARD
WINNING
Magazine

Meet

The Missing Marble Case

Gore Vale mansion, 1925

BOYS CLUB

Many years ago, in 1925, a boy stood on the porch of Gore Vale mansion (see left) with his friends. As he played with a marble in his pocket, it fell out, rolled across the porch, and over the edge into the dirt below. There it stayed until it was found by the team of dirt detectives—over 60 years later!

the Dirt Detectives!

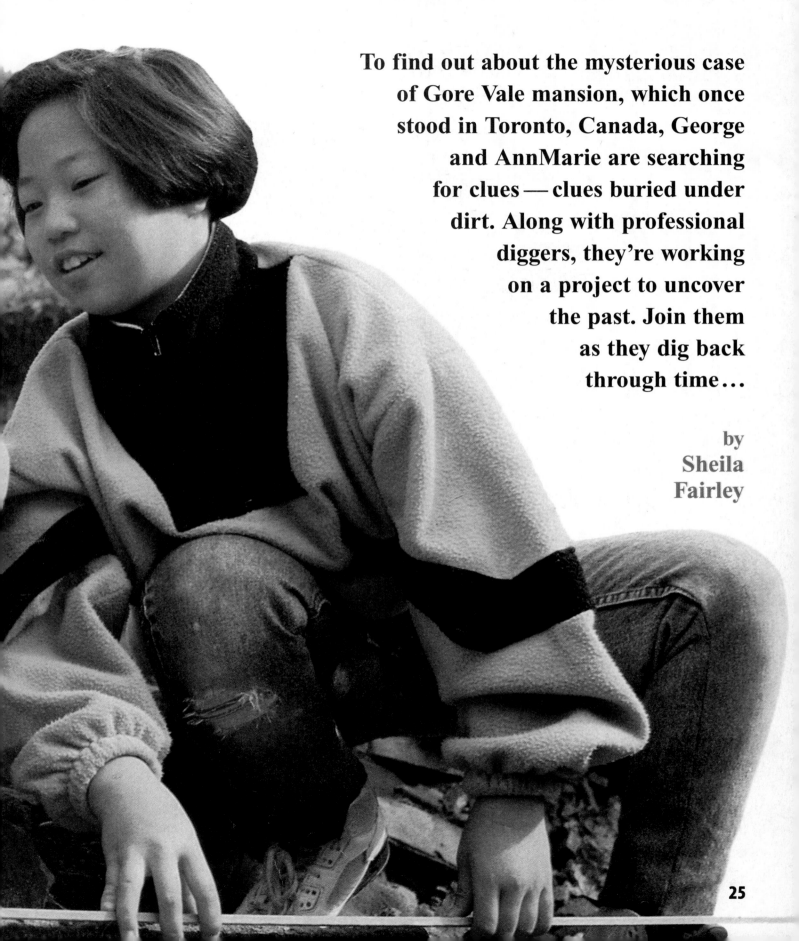

To find out about the mysterious case of Gore Vale mansion, which once stood in Toronto, Canada, George and AnnMarie are searching for clues—clues buried under dirt. Along with professional diggers, they're working on a project to uncover the past. Join them as they dig back through time…

by
Sheila
Fairley

25

OWL: How did you get interested in digging in the first place?

George: My mom told me about it and so did my uncle who's a teacher.

AnnMarie: I knew a bit about it before coming here with my class, but I had never been on a dig.

OWL: When you first came on the dig, did you have any idea of what you expected to find?

George: I didn't really think I would find anything, but I was lucky. The first day I found a nail, some brick chips and a piece of glass.

OWL: Now that you've worked on this project, has it changed the way you think about the past?

AnnMarie: Before, I thought it was boring, but now I see it's not. We have two hours for a dig but it goes by so fast, it feels like a few minutes!

Paintbrush for brushing away dirt

Trowel for digging

Meter stick for measuring things you find

Map to record details about where you're digging

Paper bag for storing things you find

Measuring tape for measuring larger things

Dustpan for collecting dirt

Whisk broom for cleaning the area you're in

1820

Gore Vale mansion is built.

OWL: What's the most interesting thing that you've found while digging?

AnnMarie: I found part of an old china dish. You could only see part of the pattern and it was very colorful.

OWL: Was it different from the kind of dishes that we use today?

AnnMarie: Yes, the china felt like plastic.

OWL: Is there something about digging that you don't like?

George: You have to wait for a long time and you have to go slowly. I would like to be able to go a little faster.

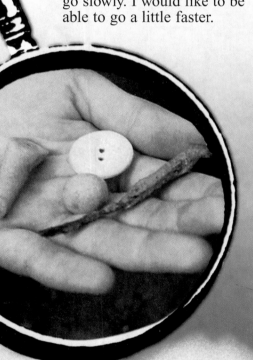

Imagine travelling to another planet and discovering these objects. What do you think they could be used for?

OWL: If you could leave something behind for future diggers to find, what would it be?

AnnMarie: Clothes . . . baggy jeans, and polo shirts.

George: I would probably write a letter or bury a time capsule. I'd write about the things we do.

OWL: What's the most important thing you'd like to share with OWL readers about digging?

George: Don't dig anywhere without checking because it may be against the law—and it could be dangerous!

AnnMarie: If you get a chance, try it—it's really fun. You have to wait, you have to be patient and you never know when something's going to turn up. But when it does, it's a surprise.

1925
Gore Vale is turned into a boy's club and then torn down.

1946
Family housing is built where Gore Vale once stood.

TODAY
Dirt detectives at work!

Dr. Ruben Mendoza

Archaeologist

Archaeology is *fun*. Can *you* dig it?

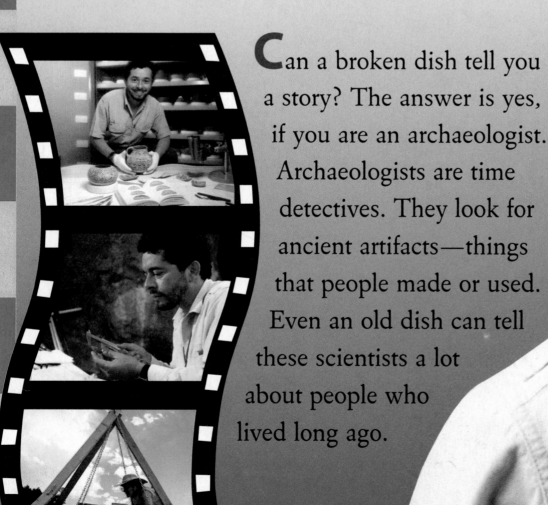

Can a broken dish tell you a story? The answer is yes, if you are an archaeologist. Archaeologists are time detectives. They look for ancient artifacts—things that people made or used. Even an old dish can tell these scientists a lot about people who lived long ago.

PROFILE

Name: Dr. Ruben Mendoza

Born: French Camp, California

Job: assistant professor of archaeology at the University of Colorado

Hobbies: travel and photography

Most exciting find: arrowheads found near Denver, Colorado, that are about 11,000 years old

Where he would go if he were a time traveler: back in time 1,400 years to an ancient city in Mexico

QUESTIONS

for Dr. Ruben Mendoza

Here's *how* **one** time detective, ***Dr. Ruben Mendoza,*** finds *clues* to the *past.*

 Q How did you become interested in archaeology?

 A I went on a trip to Mexico when I was twelve. I became fascinated by the pyramids there. Being Mexican-American, I thought about the forgotten people who had built them. I even wondered if one of my ancestors had worked on them.

 Q Weren't you recently on an archaeological trip in Mexico?

 A Yes, I went with a group of archaeologists and students. We were on a dig. We use that word because we dig up things from the past.

 Q What is the first thing you do on a dig?

 A Before we do any digging, we lay a grid of string over the whole area. Then we make a paper map showing the same thing. That way, we can record on the map where each artifact is found.

How do you know where to start digging?

 We look for clues. We might start at a circle of stones that could be the remains of an old fireplace. Or we might dig into a mound—a small hill. This could be a spot where people left things behind.

 What do you learn from clues found on a dig?

 Sometimes we find stone knives and bone needles. These show that ancient people knew how to make and use tools.

 Are all artifacts found underground?

 No. Sometimes we find petroglyphs. They're drawings, usually found on a rock cliff or on the wall of a cave. They often picture animals that lived in the area.

 What do you do with artifacts you find on a dig?

 Each artifact is given a number, then weighed and measured. Drawings and maps are photographed. We write all these facts on a card, along with the date, place, and name of the person who found it. Later, this information goes into a computer file so it's easy for others to study. The artifacts themselves end up in a museum.

Dr. Ruben Mendoza's
Tips for Young Archaeologists

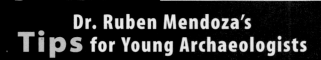

1 If you find an artifact, record exactly where you found it.

2 Study the place where you discovered the artifact. Read about the people who once might have lived there.

3 Give the artifact to a museum. Take along the records you have kept.

31

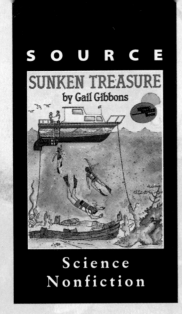

from

SUNKEN

by Gail Gibbons

"It's there! It's really there!"

The rotting hull of a ship has been found on the ocean floor. Within the wreck lies a fabulous treasure.

The story of each underwater treasure hunt is different, but each goes back to the same beginning . . . the sinking of a ship. The story of the hunt for the *Nuestra Señora de Atocha*, a Spanish galleon, begins the same way.

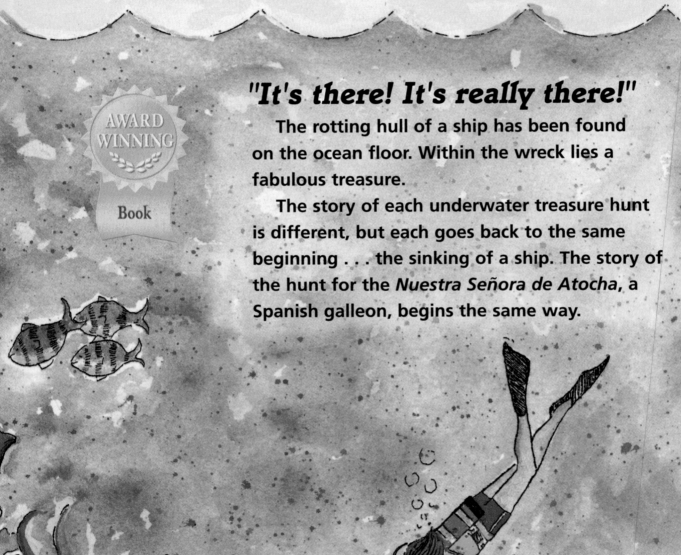

THE ATOCHA

The Sinking

It is 1622. The *Atocha*, with its fleet of sister ships, makes its way back from South America to Spain. The *Atocha* is a treasure ship, laden with gold, jewels, silver bars, and thousands of coins.

The fleet makes a stop in Cuba and then sets off again. As the ships near Florida, a hurricane gathers strength.

Wind rips at the *Atocha*'s sails. Spray washes across the deck. The 265 people aboard the ship are terrified. Suddenly, a huge wave lifts the ship and throws it against a reef.

The hull breaks open, and the *Atocha*—along with several of its sister ships—sinks beneath the waves. All but five aboard the *Atocha* drown.

The Search

Spain wants its treasure back. Search ships are sent out. They find one of the *Atocha*'s sister ships, the *Santa Margarita*, and salvage begins. Sponge and pearl divers bring some of the *Santa Margarita*'s treasure to the surface.

But the *Atocha* cannot be found.

Hundreds of years go by. The *Atocha* is almost forgotten. Storms and strong sea currents scatter its treasure for miles along the ocean floor. The ship slowly rots and breaks into pieces. Sand covers the remains.

In the early 1960's, a new search begins. A man named Mel Fisher has read about the *Atocha*. He is determined to find the lost treasure ship. He will need boats, crew, and equipment. Investors provide the money, and the venture gets under way.

Search boats go to where it is believed the *Atocha* went down.

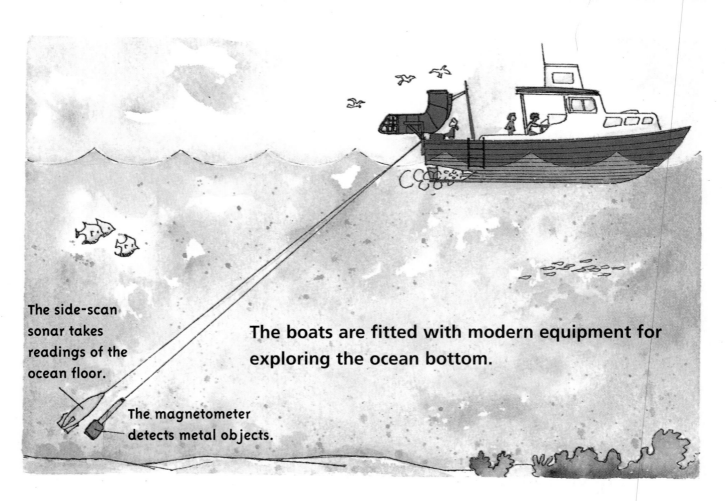

The side-scan sonar takes readings of the ocean floor.

The magnetometer detects metal objects.

The boats are fitted with modern equipment for exploring the ocean bottom.

When the instruments register a "hit," divers go down to investigate. They keep in view of each other and regularly check their air supplies.

air tank

The underwater metal detector locates metal objects, too.

Large elbow-shaped pipes, called mailboxes, are swung into place. The mailboxes are Mel Fisher's invention. The whirling of the boat's propellers forces water through the mailboxes, blowing large holes in the sand. If anything is buried, it will be uncovered.

But only litter is found—nothing of value, nothing from the *Atocha*.

mailboxes

Where should they look next?

Mel Fisher asks for help from Eugene Lyon, an expert who can translate old Spanish documents. Lyon looks through stacks of shipping records from the 1600's. The work takes years.

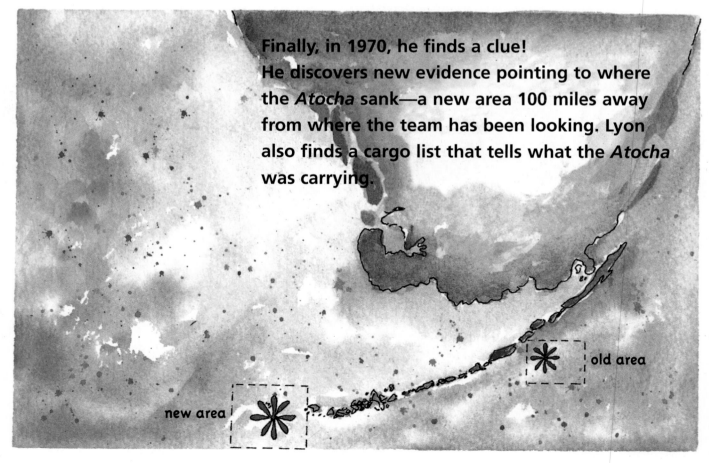

Finally, in 1970, he finds a clue!
He discovers new evidence pointing to where the *Atocha* sank—a new area 100 miles away from where the team has been looking. Lyon also finds a cargo list that tells what the *Atocha* was carrying.

old area

new area

A search boat moves to the new location.

In 1971, a huge galleon anchor, several muskets, and gold bars and chains are found. But are they from the *Atocha*? There is no way to prove it.

Two years later, three heavy silver bars are recovered. The bars with their markings match up with the *Atocha*'s cargo list. Now they have proof!

Then, in 1975, the *Atocha*'s bronze cannons are found. The crew believe they are getting closer to the mother lode . . . the main treasure of the ship.

But they are wrong. Day after day they search the huge area. Many more years go by. Crew members leave and new ones sign on. When the money runs out, new investors must be found.

1985. The crew go back and search a site they had searched years ago. And then it happens—a big "hit" registers on their equipment. Divers go down.

"We found it! The mother lode!"

Mel Fisher's twenty-year search is finally over. Resting on the ocean floor, 55 feet below, is the *Atocha*'s fabled treasure—glinting gold bars, jewelry, gold and silver coins, and other precious finds. Nearly all the listed cargo is there, and more—some treasure must have been smuggled aboard.

The Recording

The crew works with a marine archaeologist, Duncan Mathewson. He insists that the mother lode not be disturbed. A grid of plastic pipes is laid over the site.

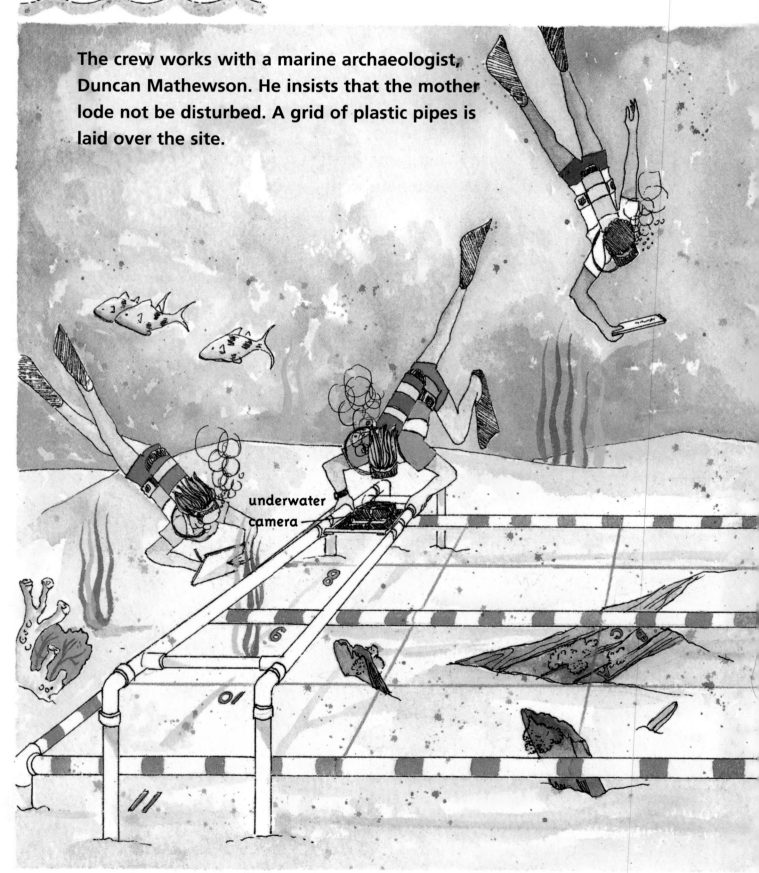

underwater camera

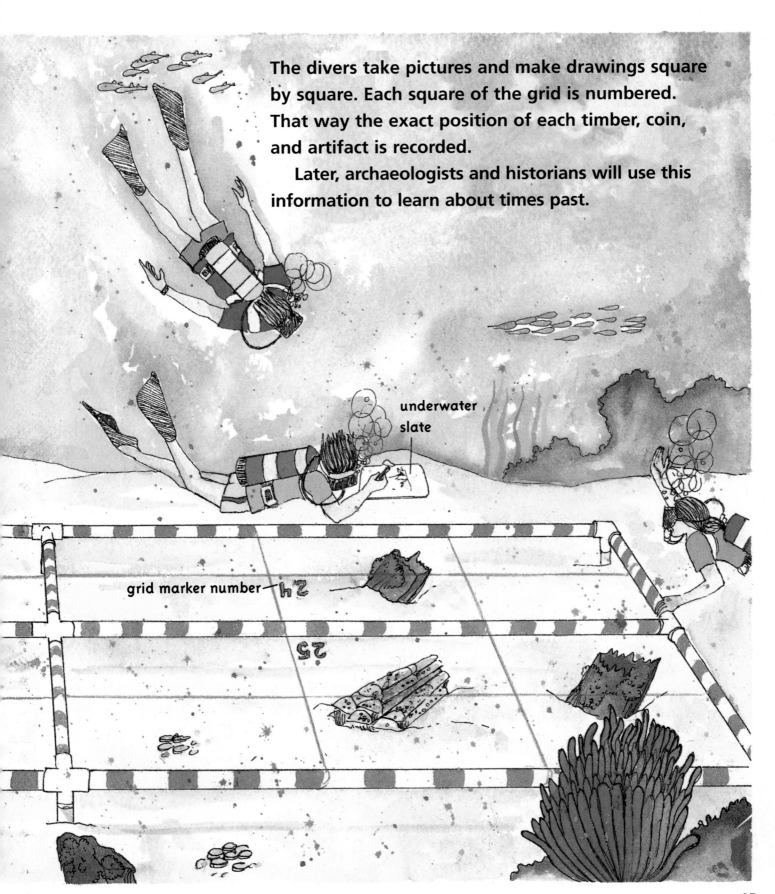

The divers take pictures and make drawings square by square. Each square of the grid is numbered. That way the exact position of each timber, coin, and artifact is recorded.

Later, archaeologists and historians will use this information to learn about times past.

underwater slate

grid marker number

The Salvage

Now the treasure can be brought to the surface.
Salvage boats are moved in. Divers descend
and crew members lower baskets over the side
to them.

The divers gently fan the sand with their hands
and use an airlift to carefully suck it away.

airlift

As treasure is recovered, other artifacts are exposed underneath. Each piece of treasure must be accounted for. Again, everything found is sketched and photographed.

One after another, baskets full of treasure are raised to the surface.

Each day the work continues . . . dive after dive after dive. More treasure is recovered from the deep. It is hard work and can be done only in good weather.

The salvage goes on for weeks, months, and years.

Restoration and Preservation

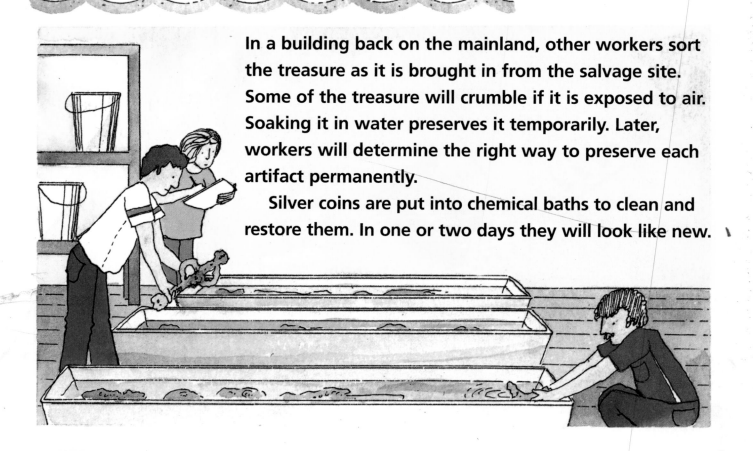

In a building back on the mainland, other workers sort the treasure as it is brought in from the salvage site. Some of the treasure will crumble if it is exposed to air. Soaking it in water preserves it temporarily. Later, workers will determine the right way to preserve each artifact permanently.

Silver coins are put into chemical baths to clean and restore them. In one or two days they will look like new.

Silver bars soak in chemical baths, too, but they will take longer to clean. They are bigger. The gold from the *Atocha* is already shiny—gold never loses its luster.

There were many pottery storage jars on board the *Atocha*. Amazingly, some are recovered whole. Other jars had been shattered and now must be pieced together again.

Cataloging

Cataloging of the *Atocha's* treasure is done in several ways:

A photographer takes pictures of a sword.

Coins are scanned by a computer, and an exact description of each one is stored in the computer's memory.

An artist draws pictures of a gold plate and an emerald-studded necklace.

This kind of careful cataloging provides a valuable record for the future.

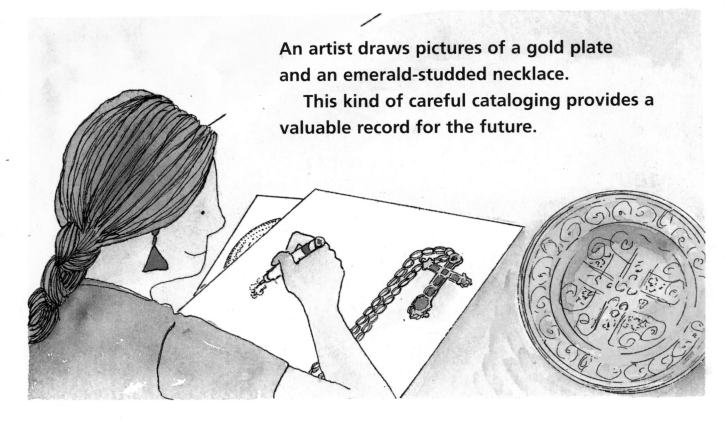

Distribution

Some of the treasure will go to museums.

Some will go to the investors and some will go to the crew. All of them made it possible for Mel Fisher's long search to continue. A computer works out what each one's fair share will be.

The treasure of the *Nuestra Señora de Atocha* is valued at hundreds of millions of dollars . . . a very wealthy treasure ship indeed!

The wreck and its artifacts will be studied by historians and archaeologists for years to come. Their discoveries will enrich our knowledge of the past. This will be the second treasure of the *Atocha*.

How to Create an Artifact Exhibit Card

artifact described in the card

How do you learn about the past? One way is to look at artifacts in a museum. You might discover a toy from ancient Egypt or an arrowhead made thousands of years ago. To learn more about each artifact, you can read the exhibit card that goes with it.

What is an exhibit card? An exhibit card gives information about an artifact—when it was made, who made it, what it was made of, and how it was used.

name of
artifact

size

ARMOR OF GEORGE CLIFFORD, THIRD EARL OF CUMBERLAND

Blued steel decorated with gold designs

Made in Greenwich, England, sometime between 1580 and 1585

Height: 69½ inches

The third earl of Cumberland wore this armor when he attended tournaments. At the tournaments, knights showed off their skills. This fancy armor was made for him at the royal armor shops in Greenwich. When the earl dressed in his armor, he had to put on fourteen different pieces. They were held together with leather straps. Each piece was made of strong plates of steel held together with metal pins. This made the armor flexible, so the earl could move easily.

This armor was purchased by the Muncie Fund in 1932.

materials
used

where
and when
artifact
was
made

description—
includes
interesting
details

information about how the museum acquired the artifact

1 Choose an Artifact

Think of all the different kinds of "artifacts" you use in a day, at home or at school. They might be for eating, traveling, doing schoolwork, playing sports, or getting ready for bed. They might be in-line skates, a fancy pencil, or a baseball cap. Choose an artifact that you would like to see in a museum.

TOOLS

- paper and pencil
- large index card
- an artifact

2 Collect Information

Gather as much information as you can about your artifact. What is it? How is it used? Where was it made? Where is it used? What is it made of? Who uses it? Is there anything unusual about it? Does it have any decorations? Keep notes on your discoveries.

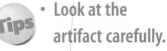

Tips
- Look at the artifact carefully.
- Think of what you already know about it.
- Read labels and any writing on it.
- Read about it in a reference book.

3 Write Your Card

Use the information you've gathered to write your exhibit card.

- On the index card, write the artifact's name.
- Below the name, write a short paragraph about the artifact.
- Include interesting facts.

Place your artifact with its exhibit card.

4 Create an Exhibit

With your classmates, set up a museum exhibit called "Things We Use." Put artifacts that are similar together. For example, artifacts about school might go in one group. Artifacts about hobbies might go in another. Display each artifact with its exhibit card. Now tour your museum. Look at all the artifacts. What did you discover about the time you live in?

If You Are Using a Computer ...

Create your exhibit card using the Poster format. Browse through the collection of clip art for an artifact to show on your card. Choose an attractive border to make your card complete.

THINK

Imagine that you could travel a hundred years into the future. What artifacts from today do you think you might find?

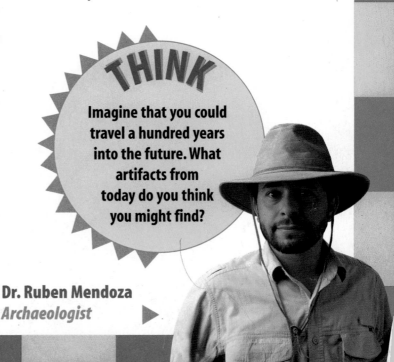

Dr. Ruben Mendoza
Archaeologist ▶

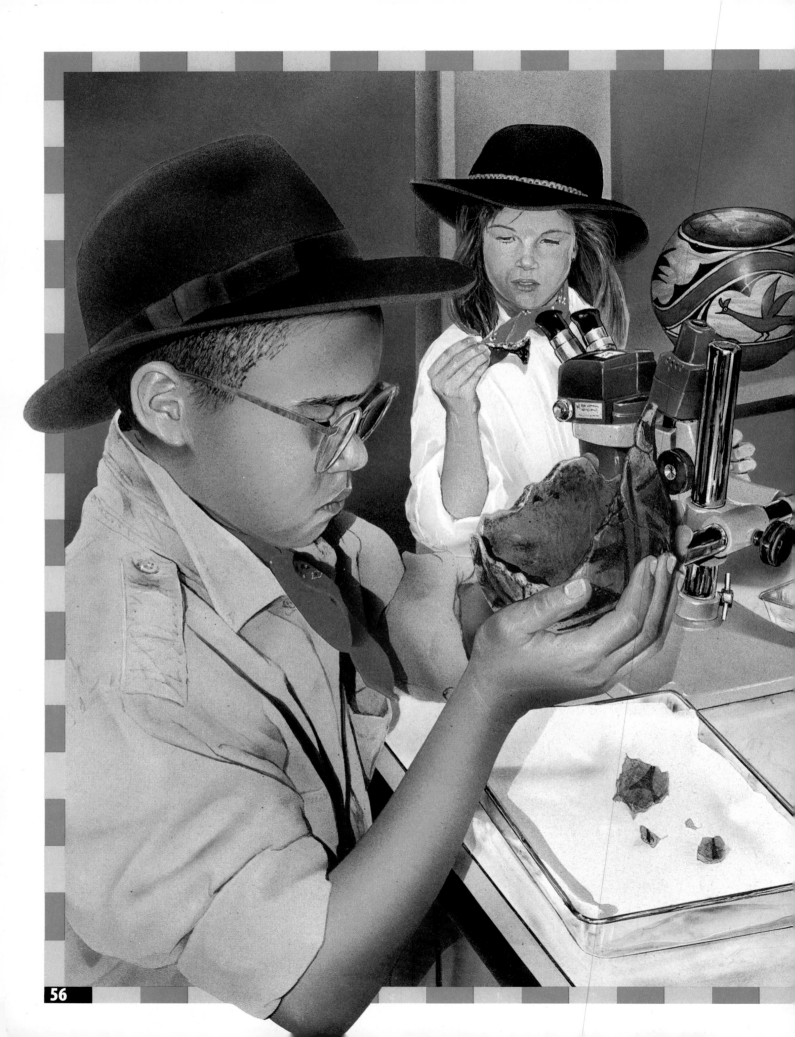

Look at the Clues

Discover what
26 amazing
artifacts—from
A to Z—tell us
about the past.

Meet a
young Pueblo
storyteller
and share
her favorite
legend about
her people.

WORKSHOP 2

Search for clues to the past in
an old picture.

CLUES
to the
PAST

A *to* Z

by

Patricia and Fredrick McKissack

AWARD WINNING

Authors

This is a book of artifacts. An artifact is an object from the past that can tell us something about the people who made and used it.

Follow the alphabet from A to Z to learn about 26 artifacts and their stories.

Happy exploring!

Arrowhead

Long ago, people used bows and arrows to hunt and wage war. They usually made arrowheads from materials such as shells, rocks, and bones found near their homes. Native Americans west of the Rocky Mountains probably shaped these arrowheads. The rocks they're made from are plentiful there.

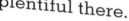

Basket

Baskets were among the first objects people learned to make. They were beautiful as well as useful. These sea grass baskets were woven by African Americans. Their slave ancestors brought the art of basket making from Africa. They passed the skill down to their children and grandchildren.

Coin

Coins often give us information about the past. This one-dollar coin was issued between 1979 and 1981 by the United States government. It honors Susan B. Anthony. During the 19th century, she worked for an end to slavery and for the right of women to vote.

Doll

We know that children have played with dolls for the last 3,000 years. This doll was found in an ancient Egyptian tomb. It gives us an idea of how Egyptian children dressed and wore their hair long ago.

Eyeglasses

This painting of Benjamin Franklin tells us an interesting story about eyeglasses. The famous inventor is wearing bifocals, which are special glasses that he designed in 1784.

Fabric

Long ago in Scotland, all the great families wore clothing made from specially designed fabric called tartan. You could tell which family a person belonged to by the tartan he or she wore. Today, Scots still wear their family tartan. But tartan plaids have also become popular with people all over the world.

Game

Yes, children played jacks and marbles over 3,000 years ago. Knucklebones was the ancient Greek form of jacks. And Roman children played with colored glass and pottery marbles.

Hat

the last drop from his STETSON

In the American West, the cowboy's hat was more than a fashion craze. Cowboys used their hats to water their horses, and also as fans, umbrellas, drinking cups, and even as pillows.

Ice skates

Ice skates like these were popular with Americans in the 1860s. The ankle strap was a new addition at that time. It helped people keep their balance.

Journal

Many travelers keep journals. Journals help us see a place as the traveler saw it. Meriwether Lewis and William Clark explored the land northwest of the Mississippi River between 1804 and 1806. Each of them kept a journal.

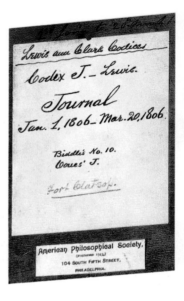

Kite

The Chinese were the first to make and fly kites. Their kites help us learn about Chinese culture and traditions. The Chinese flew kites to celebrate births, marriages, holidays, and festivals. The butterfly kite is one of the oldest and most popular designs.

Lamp

In the 1800s, before electric lights were invented, many people used gas lamps to light their homes. Gas lamps were also used to light the streets at night.

Map

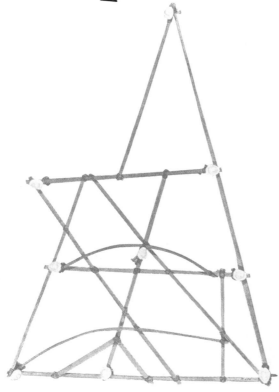

Long ago, people from the Marshall Islands made very accurate maps from grass reeds and sea shells. They used these maps to travel from island to island in the huge Pacific Ocean. Each cowrie shell marks the location of an island. The reed sticks show the direction of the waves between the islands.

Newspaper

Old newspapers are a great source of information about the past. *The New York Times* began publishing in 1851. It has kept a running diary of the day-to-day activities of ordinary and extraordinary people since the first day it went to press. What were the headlines on the day *you* were born?

Olla

For hundreds of years, Native Americans of the Southwest made clay jars called *ollas* (OH-yuz) to carry water to their homes. Ollas are still being made. Today they are sometimes used as water jars. But more often, they are collected as beautiful works of art.

Portrait

Every American president has been painted or photographed. Abraham Lincoln's portraits are among the most well known. These two photographs show how much he changed from the time he took office in 1861 until his death in 1865.

◀ 1861

1865 ▶

Quilt

This bride's quilt, from the 1850s, shows scenes from the bride's life. It tells the personal story of her courtship, engagement, and even her hopes and dreams for the future. When quilts are passed down from one generation to another, so are their stories.

Rug

The desert nomads of Persia were among the earliest known rug makers. They used their beautiful rugs in their daily lives. Persian carpets became very popular in Europe in the 1400s. Europeans used the one-of-a-kind rugs as wall hangings or table covers. They rarely used them on the floor!

Sundial

How did people tell time before there were clocks or watches? They often used sundials—sometimes portable ones like this one! The position of the sun's shadow on the dial showed the time. What happened when it was cloudy? People made a good guess.

Toy

Teddy bears are one of the best-loved toys in the world. They were named after President Theodore "Teddy" Roosevelt. In 1902, toymaker Morris Michtom saw a cartoon showing the President unwilling to shoot a bear cub. He made the toy teddy bear to honor the President.

Umbrella

The umbrella is an item we use to keep dry in the rain. But for the Asante people of West Africa, the umbrella was—and still is—a symbol of the king's power. There were hundreds of royal umbrellas. Each one had a special meaning. For example, when a king sat under an umbrella topped with a hen and baby chicks, it meant he was a judge settling arguments.

Vacuum cleaner

This is not an early fire engine! It's the original vacuum cleaner, invented in England in 1901. Men in uniform pulled it down city streets and offered to vacuum people's rugs. The machine remained on the street, and the hose was put through a window.

Weathervane and Whirligig

For many centuries people have wanted to know, "Which way is the wind blowing and how fast?" Long before there were TV weather forecasters, people put weathervanes and whirligigs on poles, rooftops, fences, and mailboxes to keep track of wind direction and speed. Today these objects are often used as decorations.

X-chair

The X-chair is one of the oldest kinds of folding furniture. The ancient Egyptians and Romans were the first to use X-chairs. They were easy for soldiers and hunters to carry. Later, European furniture makers called the X-chair a "scissor chair." Can you see why?

Yarn painting

The Huichol people of Mexico are known for their colorful yarn paintings. Each picture shows things that are important to the Huichol way of life—the sun, corn, sheep. For hundreds of years, these beautiful designs were painted or carved on rocks. Then the Huichol began to make their pictures with yarn.

Zither

Zithers were first made in China thousands of years ago. Different designs spread all over the world. During the early 1700s, zithers like this one were brought to America by European immigrants. The zither is one of the instruments that gives Appalachian music its twangy sound.

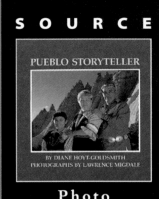
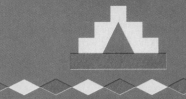

from

Pueblo Storyteller

BY **DIANE HOYT-GOLDSMITH**
PHOTOGRAPHS BY **LAWRENCE MIGDALE**

My name is April. I live with my grandparents in the Cochiti (KOH-chi-tee) Pueblo near Santa Fe, New Mexico. Pueblo (PWEB-loh) is a Spanish word that means "village" or "town." Our pueblo is very old. The Cochiti people have lived on these lands for many hundreds of years.

For me there is a special time at the end of every day. After the work is finished and I am ready to go to bed, my grandmother and grandfather tell me stories from the past. Sometimes they tell about the legends of the pueblo people. Other times they tell about things that happened in their own lives.

My grandmother likes to tell about when she was a girl. She lived in a Tewa (*TAY-wah*) pueblo to the north called San Juan. She remembers autumn, a time when her whole family worked together to harvest and husk the corn crop. The corn came in many colors—red and orange, yellow and white, blue and purple, and even the deepest black.

Her family would sit in the shade of a ramada (*rah-MAH-dah*) built of cedar branches. Sheltered from the hot sun, the workers would remove the husks from a mountain of colorful corn. All the time they were working, they would laugh at jokes, sing songs, and share stories.

My grandmother tells me there were always lots of children around—her brothers and sisters, their cousins and friends—and they always had fun. My grandfather tells how the boys would use their slingshots to hurl stones at the crows who came too close to the corncobs that were drying in the sun.

As I listen to their stories, I can almost hear the sound of laughter as the children play at their games. I can smell the bread baking as the women prepare to feed their families. I can see the mounds of corn, colored like the rainbow, drying in the sun.

When I was very young, my grandparents told me a legend about how our ancestors found the place where we are living today, our pueblo along the Rio Grande River. They call it "How the People Came to Earth," and it is still one of my favorite tales.

How the People Came to Earth

◀◀◀◀◀◆▶▶▶▶▶

A PUEBLO LEGEND

Long, long ago, our people wandered from place to place across the universe. Their leader was Long Sash, the star that we call Orion. He was the great warrior of the skies. Long Sash told his people that he had heard of a land far away, a place where they could make a home.

Because the people were weary of wandering, they decided to follow Long Sash on the dangerous journey across the sky to search for a new home. They traveled on the Endless Trail, the river of countless stars that we call the Milky Way.

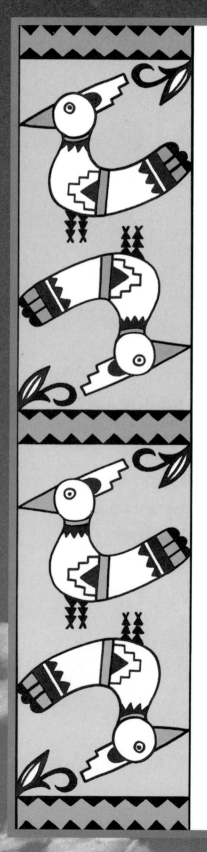

The way was hard for our people. Long Sash taught them to hunt for food, and to make clothing from the skins of animals and the feathers of birds. Even so, they were often hungry and cold, and many died along the way. Long Sash led them farther than any people had ever gone before.

After a time, the people came to a vast darkness, and they were afraid. But Long Sash, the great warrior, believed they were heading the right way, and led them on. Suddenly, they heard the faint sound of scratching. Then, as they watched, a tiny speck of light appeared in the distance. As they got nearer, the light grew larger and larger. Then they saw that it was a small hole leading to another world.

When they looked through the opening, they saw a little mole digging away in the earth. Long Sash thanked the mole for helping them to find their way out of the darkness. But the mole only replied, "Come in to our world. And when you see the sign of my footprints again, you will know you have found your true home." The people saw a cord hanging down from the hole and they all climbed up and went through into the new world.

Once through the opening, Long Sash saw Old Spider Woman busily weaving her web. He asked permission to pass through her house. Old Spider Woman replied, "You may come through my house. But when you next see the sign of my spiderweb, you will have found your true home."

The people did not understand what Old Spider Woman meant, but they thanked her and continued on their journey.

Long Sash and his followers traveled to many places on the earth. They found lands of ice and snow, lands where the sun burned and the air was dry, and beautiful lands with tall trees and plenty of game for hunting. In all of these places, they searched for signs of the mole and Old Spider Woman, but found nothing.

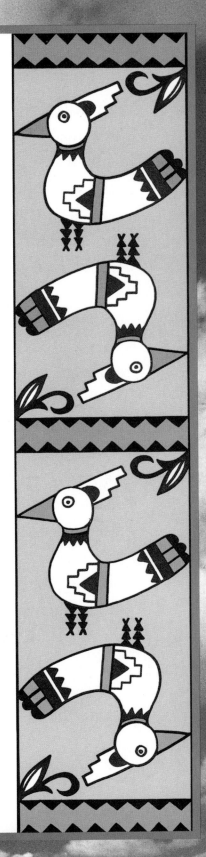

Some of the people stayed behind in the lands they discovered, but Long Sash and most of the tribe kept going. They kept searching for their true home.

Finally they came to a new land where the seasons were wet and dry, hot and cold, with good soil and bad. They found, here and there, small tracks that looked like a mole's. They followed the tracks and found a strange-looking creature, with ugly, wrinkled skin. The slow-moving animal carried a rounded shell on its back.

Long Sash was very happy when he saw the creature. "Look!" he said. "He carries his home with him, as we have done these many years. He travels slowly, just like us. On his shell are the markings of the spiderweb and his tracks look just like the mole's."

When our people saw the turtle, they knew they had found the homeland they had traveled the universe to discover. And we still live on those same lands today.

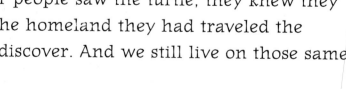

My grandparents are storytellers who have brought the past alive for me through their memories, through their language, through their art, and even through the food we eat. I am thankful that they have given me this rich history. From them I have learned to bake bread in an ancient way, to work with the earth's gift of clay, and to dance to the music of the Cochiti drums.

I am a pueblo child and I love to listen to my grandparents tell stories. From their example, I learn to take what I need from the earth to live, but also how to leave something behind for future generations. Every day I am learning to live in harmony with the world. And every day, I am collecting memories of my life to share one day with my own children and grandchildren.

How to Discover Picture Clues

How can we learn about people who lived 50, 100, or even 500 years ago? One way is to look for picture clues in old paintings or photographs.

What are picture clues? Picture clues are the details you see in paintings and photographs. These special clues show what life was like long ago—how people dressed, how they traveled, what they ate, and even what they did for fun.

Clothing was different from that worn by people today.

Horses were used for transportation.

The one-room schoolhouse was made of logs.

There were no other buildings nearby.

The children were different ages.

In Colorado during the late 1800s, children rode horses to school every day. Students in grades 1 through 8 all studied together in a one-room log cabin—and one teacher taught them all.

The caption tells about the photo.

1 Find a Picture

In your library, find an old picture with lots of details. It can be a photograph, a drawing, or a painting. Look in books and magazines. If you need help, ask your librarian. Or ask your family to find an old picture at home.

TOOLS

- old painting or photograph
- notebook
- pencil
- magnifying glass (optional)

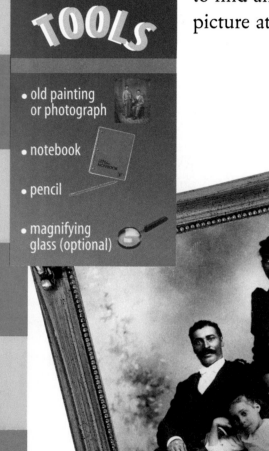

2 Look for Clues

Look carefully at your picture. Take notes on what you see. These questions may help you.

- When was the picture taken?
- What place does it show?
- Who are the people in the picture?
- What are they wearing?
- What are they doing?

Do you notice anything else—toys, food, furniture, kinds of transportation?

3 Organize Your Notes

Scientists like Dr. Ruben Mendoza organize their notes. It helps them write about what they have found. You can use a chart to organize your notes about the old picture you looked at.

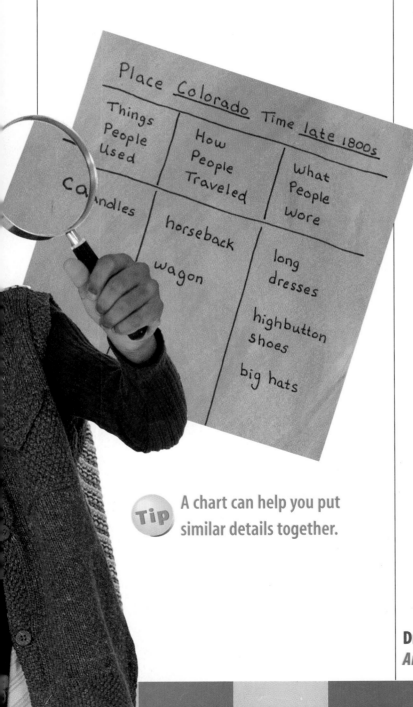

Tip A chart can help you put similar details together.

4 Write a Caption

Now you can tell the world about the picture you chose. Look at your notes and chart. Decide which details are most important. Then write an informational caption that tells what is happening in the picture. Share the picture and caption with your classmates. Tell them what you discovered about the past.

If You Are Using a Computer...

Use your Newsletter format on the computer to make your organizing chart. Create columns and headings to help order your notes. If you like, you may also write the caption for your picture using a special font.

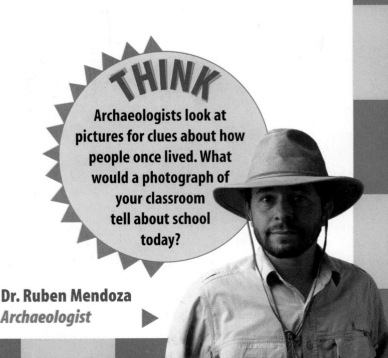

THINK

Archaeologists look at pictures for clues about how people once lived. What would a photograph of your classroom tell about school today?

Dr. Ruben Mendoza
Archaeologist ▶

We can piece together a picture of the past by adding up the evidence.

Add Up the Evidence

Learn what life was like at the time of the great woolly mammoths.

Find out what a time capsule reveals about life 75 years ago.

Discover what tomorrow's children might think about life today.

PROJECT

Make your own time capsule for future archaeologists.

FROM

WILD AND WOOLLY MAMMOTHS

BY ALIKI

AWARD WINNING
Author

Mammoths were the giant land mammals of their time.

They roamed quietly in groups.

Mammoths were peaceful plant eaters.

They did not have to hunt other animals for food.

But they had enemies.

One was the fierce saber-toothed tiger.

There were other enemies, too.
Man was the mammoth's greatest enemy.
Inside dark, damp caves scientists found out
   how important the mammoth was to early man.

They discovered paintings of mammoths on cave walls.

They found clay figures and bone carvings of mammoths and other animals.

They knew no animal made them.

They were made by early people who lived in the caves.

They were made in the days of the mammoth hunters, more than 25,000 years ago.

These hunters used tools made of stone, so we call their time the Stone Age.

These are some of the things found in caves in France.

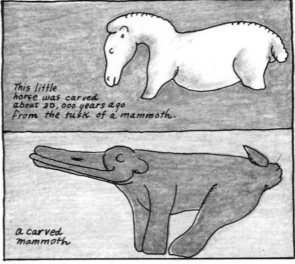

Bone knife carved with bison and plants.

This little horse was carved about 30,000 years ago from the tusk of a mammoth.

a carved mammoth

Woolly mammoth carved in stone

A whole Stone Age village was found in Czechoslovakia and dug up.

Archaeologists, who are scientists who study ancient ruins, learned a lot from this village and others like it.

They learned more about mammoth hunters and how they lived.

This is what they found out.

Mammoth hunters left the caves where they lived in the winter.

In the spring they moved to river valleys where herds of
   mammoths roamed.

They made tents in the valleys to be near the mammoths.

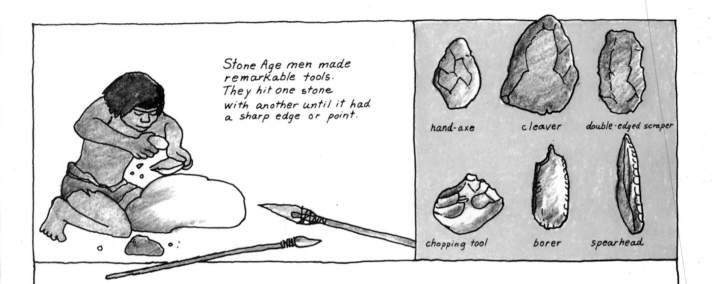

Stone Age men made remarkable tools. They hit one stone with another until it had a sharp edge or point.

hand-axe   cleaver   double-edged scraper

chopping tool   borer   spearhead

The mammoth hunters made knives and other tools of stone.
They used wooden spears with sharp stone points to kill the
   mammoths.
But first they had to trap them.
Sometimes the hunters made fires around the herds.
Then they forced the frightened mammoths down steep cliffs.
Other hunters waited at the bottom to kill the mammoths with
   their spears.

Sometimes the mammoth
hunters dug deep pits.
They covered the pits with
branches and earth.

When a mammoth
walked over the pit,
the branches broke,
and the mammoth fell in.

It could not escape.
Hunters rolled heavy stones
down on it and killed the
trapped mammoth.

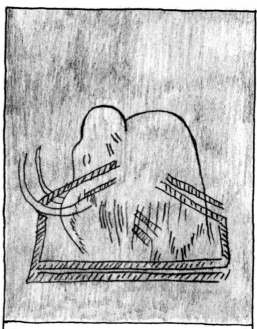

Many mammoths found showed that
their bones had been broken.

This Stone Age painting
was found on a wall
in a cave in France.

Some people think
it shows a mammoth
caught in a pit trap.

The hunters and their families ate the mammoth meat.
They crushed the skulls and ate the brains.

They used the bones to
make tent frames.

They burned bones
for fuel, too.

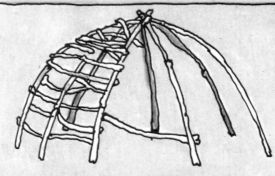

Then the bones were probably covered
with the skins of other animals.

The fat from inside the bones
oozed out and kept the fire burning.

They used bones and tusks
to make jewelry.

The earliest musical
instruments we know about
were made of mammoths'
bones and tusks.
But their skin was too tough
for anything.

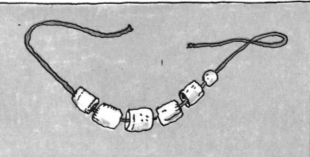

Necklace beads found in Czechoslovakia
were carved from mammoth tusks.

These people hunted other animals, too.
The woolly rhinoceros and the giant sloth lived then.

Today they are extinct.

But bison, reindeer, horses, and foxes, which also lived then, have not died out.

Mammoths were hunted for a long time.

There were plenty of them, and one mammoth was enough to feed many families.

Today there are no mammoths.

Some people think it was the mammoth hunters who killed them all.

Perhaps they died out when the climate grew too warm.

No one knows.

But not one live woolly mammoth has been seen for 11,000 years.

SOURCE

Cricket
Magazine

MY FATHER'S GRANDFATHER  AND THE  TIME MACHINE

by **Staton Rabin**

illustrated by **Gail Piazza**

Last week when the winter sky was blue like a robin's egg, we rode a rickety train into the city. The train went one way, and the seats on it faced the other. So, backwards we went, at forty miles an hour, my father's grandfather and I—rattling all the way.

"Will you hold my hand in the city?" Grandpa asked me. The train wiggled and made us sway from side to side. He whispered in my ear, "I'm afraid of the alligators."

"Well . . . O.K.," I said. "But there aren't any alligators, and you know it. *Now* will you tell me why we're going to the city?"

"We're going back in time," my father's grandfather said. "We're taking a trip in a time machine."

And that's all he would tell me until we finally stood on a
checkered stone floor inside a tall building. I was glad to be out
of the cold, but why had we come in here? There was nothing
to see or do—just a big, stone room that made my voice echo
when I talked.

"O.K., where's the time machine?" I asked impatiently.

Grandpa looked at his watch and said, "Close your eyes."

"This is silly," I told him, but I closed my eyes. He led me
somewhere by the hand and then said, "Open them."

I did, but I still didn't see a time machine—just a few old
people standing around in a group. One old man was kneeling
on the floor with a crowbar in his hand. He was prying a heavy
brass circle from the floor.

"What's he doing?" I whispered to Grandpa.

"He's opening the time capsule," he whispered back.

"Is that like a pill for when you're sick?"

"Very funny," my father's grandfather said.

With a final grunt, the old man lifted the brass circle from the floor. The others applauded and cheered in scratchy old voices. Then one of them reached into the deep hole in the floor that had been covered by the brass circle and gently lifted out a metal box. Slowly the man opened it, and we crowded around to see what was inside.

What a disappointment! There was just a bunch of old junk in the box.

"Grandpa! You brought me here to see junk?" I said a bit too loudly. "Why would anyone want to bury some junk in the floor?"

The old people turned to stare at me, and I was a little embarrassed.

"Young lady," one of the old men said to me. He wasn't smiling. "People bury a time capsule so that people who come after them, a long time after they're gone, can dig it up and learn what life was really like for them. What the world was like long ago. A time capsule says: This is who we were. This is how we want to be remembered."

"Oh," I said. "So what do you put in a time capsule?"

"Everyday things," the old man replied, wiping his nose with a large, wrinkled handkerchief.

"Like a handkerchief?"

"And why not? Ordinary things. Not-so-ordinary things. Anything that will last a while. Not what you ate for lunch today. I'd hate to be the one to dig up your tuna fish sandwich a thousand years from now."

"I had peanut butter for lunch," I said.

The old man smiled.

I turned to Grandpa. "How do you know when it's time to dig it up, Grandpa? The time capsule, I mean."

"Sometimes it's whenever people think it's time," he said. "Or when somebody notices it's there after years of not noticing. But, sometimes, the time capsule tells you when to open it."

"And this one?" I asked.

"They're going to tear this building down," he said. "So now's the time to open the capsule, don't you think?"

"What's the number on it mean?"

"That's the year the capsule was buried. Seventy-six years ago."

The old people were busily looking through the items in the box. We looked over their shoulders.

There was an old machine in it. Grandpa told me it was a radio. . . . Some newspaper clippings and an x-ray of somebody's lungs. Grandpa explained that x-rays and radios were pretty new in 1915. There was also a shoe in the box—

but not the kind you see every day—a horseshoe! There
were a few other things in the time capsule, but I was most
interested in a photograph that Grandpa had pulled from the
bottom of the box.

"See the kid in the round glasses and the short pants?" he
said, pointing to a boy in the photo.

"Pretty nerdy!" I said. "Did everyone dress like that?"

"Watch what you say about your grandpa," he said, laughing.

"Grandpa! *You* put the photo in the time capsule!"

"That's your great-great-grandma Maggie, standing next to me," he said, pointing to the tall, skinny woman in the photo. I'd never seen a picture of her before. She was my father's grandfather's mother. "And there's your great-uncle Schuyler. He was my oldest brother. I guess," he continued, "some of

these people here with us today are the sons and daughters of people who put things in the time capsule. I'm probably the only one old enough to have been around then!"

"How'd you get to put something in the capsule?" I asked him.

"Well, they had a contest in the newspaper. I had to write, in twenty-five words or less, what I'd put in the time capsule if I got the chance, and why."

"And you were one of the winners! What did you say, Grandpa?"

"It was so long ago . . . Well, I think I said, 'I want to put a photo of me and my brother and our mom in the time capsule, so that seventy-six years from now I can bring my beautiful great-granddaughter here and show her how funny . . . I mean nerdy . . . we looked.'"

"Grandpa, did you really say that?"

"Of course," he said.

"No, you didn't! That's more than twenty-five words."

Grandpa just grinned.

When we got home from the city that day, I decided I wanted to bury a time capsule of my own. Grandpa said he would help me. It would be fun deciding what to put in it. How did *I* want to be remembered? What things would show best what it's like to live in the year 1991? How long would it be before someone found it? What would the world be like then?

Mom said it would be O.K. to dig a hole in the yard—as long as I didn't dig up her rosebushes.

SOURCE

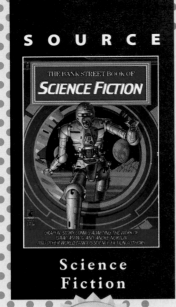

THE BANK STREET BOOK OF
SCIENCE FICTION

Science
Fiction

AWARD
WINNING

Author

from
The Bank Street Book of Science Fiction

THE FUN THEY HAD

BY ISAAC ASIMOV

Adapted by Dwight Jon Zimmerman
Illustrated by Evan Dorkin

ENTRY NAME: MARGIE
SUBJECT: DIARY
DATE: 17 MAY 2155

TODAY TOMMY FOUND A REAL BOOK. HE BROUGHT IT OVER TO SHOW ME BEFORE SCHOOL.

IT WAS CALLED SCHOOL TIME. AND IT WAS VERY OLD...

SCHOOL TIME

IT WAS AWFULLY FUNNY TO SEE WORDS THAT STAND STILL INSTEAD OF MOVING THE WAY THEY ARE SUPPOSED TO--

SCHOOL TIME

--ON A COMPUTER SCREEN!

I CAN'T BELIEVE ANYONE WOULD WANT TO WRITE ABOUT SCHOOL.

WHY NOT?

BECAUSE I HATE SCHOOL!

DIARY, SOMETIMES I *REALLY* HATE SCHOOL! LIKE LAST YEAR, WHEN I GOT SUCH BAD GRADES IN SOLAR STUDIES THAT MOM CALLED THE COUNTY INSPECTOR!

DIARY, SOME... I REALLY

I WAS HOPING THAT MY ELECTRONIC TEACHER WAS BROKEN AND COULDN'T BE FIXED.

BUT THE INSPECTOR DISCOVERED THE PROBLEM.

THE SOLAR STUDIES SECTION WAS JUST GEARED TOO FAST FOR HER, SO I HAVE REPROGRAMMED IT TO THE PROPER LEVEL.

ACTUALLY, MARGIE, YOUR OVERALL PROGRESS IS QUITE SATISFACTORY.

OH DIARY, WHAT I REALLY WANTED WAS FOR THE INSPECTOR TO TAKE MY TEACHER AWAY! BUT, BACK TO TOMMY'S BOOK...

YOU STILL HAVEN'T TOLD ME WHY ANYONE WOULD WANT TO WRITE ABOUT SCHOOL.

BECAUSE IT WASN'T OUR KIND OF SCHOOL, STUPID.

SCHOOL TIME

WELL, THEY JUST TOLD THE BOYS AND GIRLS THINGS, AND GAVE THEM HOMEWORK-- FROM BOOKS.

BUT I WOULDN'T WANT A STRANGE PERSON COMING TO MY HOUSE TO BE MY TEACHER.

YOU DON'T KNOW MUCH, MARGIE! THE TEACHERS DIDN'T COME TO YOUR HOUSE!

THERE WERE SPECIAL BUILDINGS CALLED PUBLIC SCHOOLS. KIDS THE SAME AGE WERE PUT IN GROUPS CALLED CLASSES. EVERY DAY YOU WERE ALLOWED TO GO TO SCHOOL WITH YOUR FRIENDS!

I WANTED TO READ ABOUT THOSE FUNNY SCHOOLS MYSELF, BUT MOM CAME IN.

OKAY, MARGIE--TIME FOR SCHOOL!

AS TOMMY LEFT TO GO BACK HOME, I ASKED HIM IF I COULD READ HIS BOOK AFTER SCHOOL.

TOMMY WINKED AND NODDED.

WHEN I GOT TO THE SCHOOL ROOM IN OUR BASEMENT, THE ELECTRONIC TEACHER WAS ALREADY ON AND FLASHING 1/4 + 1/2 = X.

BUT I WAS TOO EXCITED TO ADD FRACTIONS. INSTEAD I CAME HERE, TO MY COMPUTER, TO RECORD THIS STORY.

1/4 + 1/2 = X
???

Kids Predict the Future

SOURCE

SCHOLASTIC NEWS.

News Magazine

Scholastic News asked third graders around the country what they think the future will be like. Here is what some of them said.

There will be no school. We will learn from computers and robots at home.

Megan Brock
The Dalles, Oregon

Robots might do jobs that are dangerous for people and jobs like washing dishes. They could also become our friends.

Casey Allison
Baraboo, Wisconsin

Houses will have inflatable floats under them for any water emergency such as a flood or a hurricane.

Cedric Mims
Cedar Hill, Texas

Cars will be solar-powered. In the night they will be battery operated.

Jamie Sanderson
Slaterville Springs, New York

We will visit other planets. We will make friends with people on other planets. Astronauts will have to learn lots of languages to communicate with others.

Harry Gomez
Fairfax, Virginia

Looking Ahead

Here is how some children responded to a poll.

		Yes	No
1.	Will kids go to school all year long?	32	68
2.	Will you need a computer to do your job?	62	38
3.	Will we discover life in outer space?	60	40
4.	Will there be a cure for cancer?	88	12
5.	Will cats still be the most popular pet?	22	78

How to

Make a Time Capsule

***Create** a **time capsule** that tells kids in the **future** about **life** today.*

Think about this. In the future, people will study us to learn what our lives were like. Someday your neighborhood may be an archaeological site! And someone may even find a time capsule buried there. A time capsule is a container that is filled with objects and information about a certain time and place. It gets stored away to be discovered sometime in the future.

1 Gather Artifacts

What can you put into a time capsule? You can put in anything that tells about your life as a third grader. It might be an empty box from your favorite cereal, a photograph of a popular sports star, a class picture, a magazine ad for a movie you like, or a list of this week's spelling words. You might even write a diary about a day at school.

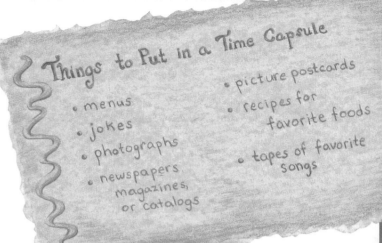

Things to Put in a Time Capsule
- menus
- jokes
- photographs
- newspapers, magazines, or catalogs
- picture postcards
- recipes for favorite foods
- tapes of favorite songs

TOOLS

- paper and pencil

- index cards

- large waterproof container made of plastic or metal

- artifacts to place into your time capsule

- clear plastic bags

- paper folder

Gather as many artifacts as you can. Now put all your artifacts into one place. Look at them closely. Decide which ones best tell about life today. These will go into your time capsule. Make a list of the artifacts you want to use.

Tips
- Place paper artifacts into clear plastic bags.
- Don't choose foods, plants, or liquids.
- Make sure objects will fit in to the time capsule.

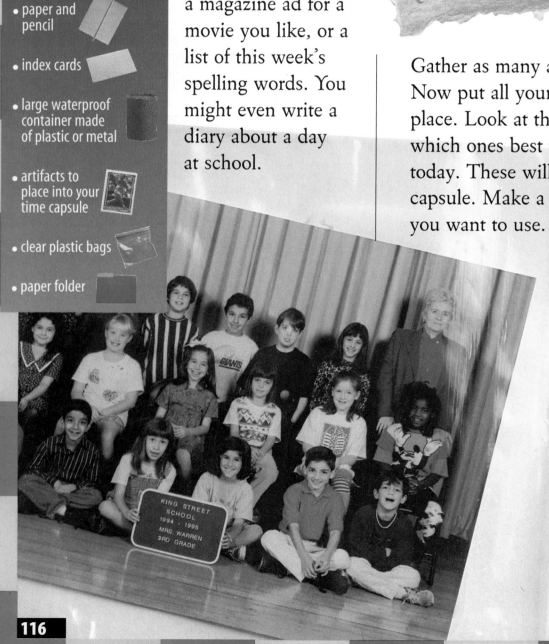

2 Label the Artifacts

You can give kids of the future more information about each artifact, too.

- Make a label for each artifact. On an index card, write the name of the artifact, what it is, and why it is important to you.

- Then tape or tie the label to the artifact.

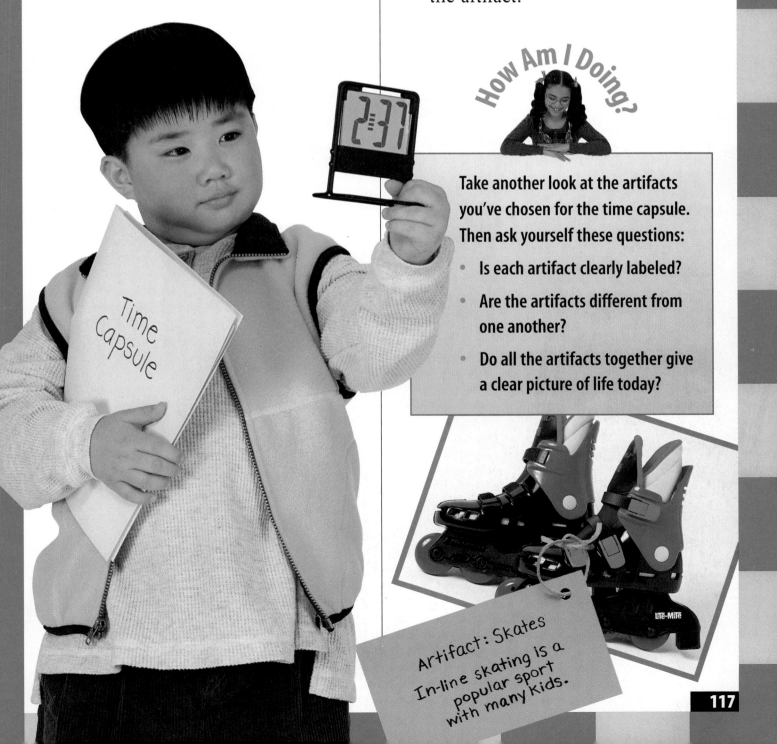

How Am I Doing?

Take another look at the artifacts you've chosen for the time capsule. Then ask yourself these questions:

- Is each artifact clearly labeled?

- Are the artifacts different from one another?

- Do all the artifacts together give a clear picture of life today?

Time Capsule

Artifact: Skates
In-line skating is a popular sport with many kids.

LiTe-MiTe

3 Greet the Future

Think of what you want to say to the kids who will open your time capsule. Write a short letter to them. Tell them about yourself. Describe what life is like today—what you like about it and what you would change.

Share your hopes for the future, too. Make a copy of your letter. Put it into a folder with your artifact list. Now you have a record of all the things you placed in your time capsule.

MILT THOMPSON   Cardinals™

4 Put the Capsule Together

Share your artifacts with the class, and tell why you chose each one. Then put your time capsule together. Carefully place your artifacts and the letter to the future inside the container you've chosen—a large plastic jar or a metal box with a tight-fitting lid. Close it up. If you like, decorate the outside of the time capsule.

When do you want your time capsule opened? In 10, 20, or even 50 years? Decide on a date in the future.

Find a place to store your time capsule. It might be in the principal's office or in your school library or in your schoolroom. Sometime in the future, another group of third graders will open it and discover what was important to you.

If You Are Using a Computer ...

Create a Journal entry on the computer about a typical day in your classroom. Then print it out to include in your time capsule. You also can write your letter to the future on the computer. Include clip art that tells about your life today.

These artifacts were collected by:

Date: Place:

Do not open until:

CONGRATULATIONS

Now you've become a real time detective. You can find clues to the past all around you. Keep looking for them!

Dr. Ruben Mendoza
Archaeologist ▶

Glossary

an·ces·tor
(an'ses tər) *noun*
A person, now dead, from whom one is descended. One *ancestor* of mine moved to America from Russia in the late 1800s.

an·cient
(ān'shənt) *adjective*
Very old or very long ago. At the museum I saw *ancient* toys that were made thousands of years ago.

Thesaurus

ancient
old
aged
antique

ar·chae·ol·o·gist
(är'kē ol'ə jist) *noun*
A person who studies people or things from a long time ago. The *archaeologist* discovered three mummies from ancient Egypt.

ar·row·heads
(ar'ō hedz') *noun*
The pointed tips of arrows. Long ago, *arrowheads* were made of sharpened stones.
▲ arrowhead

ar·ti·fact
(är'tə fact') *noun*
A tool or object made and used by people a long time ago. The archaeologist found an *artifact* that looked like a clay marble.

chim·ney
(chim'nē) *noun*
A hollow structure in a building—often made of bricks or stones—that carries away smoke from a fireplace or furnace.

chimney

clues (kloos) *noun*
Hints that help solve a problem, a mystery, or a puzzle. The footprints are *clues* that someone had walked through the yard.
▲ clue

com•put•er
(kəm pyo͞oʹtər) *noun*
An electronic machine
that can store information
and solve complicated
problems quickly.

Fact File

The first modern
machine for computing
was invented in 1946. It
weighed 30 tons, and
performed 100,000
operations per second.

e•lec•tron•ic
(i lek tronʹik) *adjective*
Having to do with
equipment such as
radios, televisions,
and computers.

foun•da•tion
(foun dāʹshən) *noun*
The bottom or base of a
building, usually below
ground. The workers
built the new house on
top of a stone *foundation*.

grid (grid) *noun*
A set of straight lines
that cross to form
squares. We drew a *grid*
over our town map so
that we could find our
friends' houses.

horse•shoe
(hôrsʹsho͞oʹ) *noun*
A flat, U-shaped metal
plate. It is nailed to the
bottom of a horse's hoof
to protect it.

jour•nals
(jûrʹnlz) *noun*
Diaries or records of
what happens each day.
▲ **journal**

leg•end (lejʹənd) *noun*
A story that is handed
down through the years.
Some or all of the story
may not be true.

Word Study

The phrase "a **legend**
in his own time," refers to
a person whose accomplish-
ments are so great that
they will be recorded in
history books.

a	add	o͞o	took	ə =
ā	ace	o͞o	pool	a in *above*
â	care	u	up	e in *sicken*
ä	palm	û	burn	i in *possible*
e	end	yo͞o	fuse	o in *melon*
ē	equal	oi	oil	u in *circus*
i	it	ou	pout	
ī	ice	ng	ring	
o	odd	th	thin	
ō	open	th	this	
ô	order	zh	vision	

Glossary

mam•moth
(mam´əth) *noun*
A large animal, like an elephant, that lived long ago. It had shaggy brown hair and long curved tusks.

Word Study

The **mammoth** was such a huge animal that people began to use its name to describe something that was large. The word **mammoth** can also mean "huge, gigantic, giant, or very large."

man•sion
(man´shən) *noun*
A very large and elegant home. The *mansion* had 30 rooms and a long driveway.

pet•ro•glyphs
(pe´trə glifs´) *noun*
Carvings or drawings on a rock. ▲ **petroglyph**

phot•o•graphs
(fō´tə grafs´) *noun*
Pictures taken with a camera. ▲ **photograph**

pueb•lo
(pweb´lō) *noun*
A Native American village that is made up of stone or adobe buildings built one above the other. Pueblos are found in the southwestern United States.

Word History

Pueblo comes from a Spanish word meaning "people" or "town." Long ago, Spanish explorers thought that Native American adobe villages in the Southwest looked like towns in Spain. The Native Americans who live in these adobe villages are also known as **Pueblo** Indians.

pyr•a•mid
(pir´ə mid) *noun*
A solid object with a flat base and triangular sides that meet at a point at the top. Some structures are built in the shape of a pyramid.

quilt (kwilt) *noun*
A bed cover made of two layers of colorful cloth with a layer of feathers or soft material between them. The stitches used to sew a *quilt* make patterns on the cloth.

re•cord (ri kôrd´) *verb*
To write down for future use. The teacher will *record* the students' test scores.

re•mem•ber
(ri mem´bər) *verb*
To bring back to mind. I *remember* my trip to Yellowstone Park last summer.

re•pro•grammed
(rē prō´gramd) *verb*
Gave new instructions to a computer about how to do its work. ▲ **reprogram**

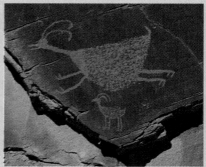

petroglyph

re•stor•a•tion (res´tə rā´shən) *noun* The act of making something like new or like it once was. After its *restoration*, the old bicycle looked brand new.

ru•ins (ro͞o´inz) *noun* Buildings that have fallen apart or have been destroyed. We visited the *ruins* of an old castle on our vacation. ▲ **ruin**

sa•ber-toothed ti•ger (sā´bər to͞otht´ tī´gər) *noun* A large animal of the cat family that lived long ago. It looked somewhat like a modern-day tiger and had long, sharp upper teeth.

sal•vage (sal´vij) *verb* To save from loss or destruction. After the flood we were able to *salvage* some of our furniture.

stores (storz) *verb* Puts away for future use. My mother *stores* cans of food in the cupboard. ▲ **store**

stor•y•tel•ler (stôr´ē tel´ər) *noun* A person who tells stories for fun or learning.

sun•di•al (sun´dī əl) *noun* An ancient kind of a clock. It shows the time of day by a shadow the sun makes on a dial.

tribe (trīb) *noun* A group of people with the same ancestors, customs, and language. The Hopi are a *tribe* of Native Americans who live in the American Southwest.

Thesaurus

tribe
clan
family
kin

tusks (tusks) *noun* Long, curving teeth. They stick out of the side of an animal's mouth. Elephants and walruses have tusks. ▲ **tusk**

sundial

a	add	o͝o	took	ə =
ā	ace	o͞o	pool	a in *above*
â	care	u	up	e in *sicken*
ä	palm	û	burn	i in *possible*
e	end	yo͞o	fuse	o in *melon*
ē	equal	oi	oil	u in *circus*
i	it	ou	pout	
ī	ice	ng	ring	
o	odd	th	thin	
ō	open	th	this	
ô	order	zh	vision	

Authors & Illustrators

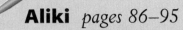

Aliki *pages 86–95*

Author/illustrator Aliki has loved to draw since she was a very little girl. In fact, her kindergarten teacher predicted she would be an artist someday. Today Aliki does more than draw. She creates books about things that interest her. She says, "Writing and illustrating books is a way of satisfying my curiosity. I'm just lucky that children are curious about the same things I am." Many of Aliki's books, such as *Wild and Woolly Mammoths* and *How a Book Is Made*, are nonfiction. She enjoys doing research and tries to make facts easy to understand. Aliki has written more than 40 books since she began her career in 1961.

Isaac Asimov *pages 104–112*

When he was just 17, Isaac Asimov sent his first science fiction story to a magazine. It was rejected! But he didn't give up and sent in another a few months later. It was accepted. Mr. Asimov went on to become a very successful science fiction writer. He wrote nonfiction books about science topics. In all, he wrote nearly 500 books! The author, who died in 1992, often wrote 18 hours a day, 7 days a week.

Gail Gibbons *pages 32–51*

This award-winning author/illustrator writes nonfiction books about the different things that interest and excite her—from how mail moves to how clocks work. She spends a lot of time doing research. Often she finds far more information than she can use. She then narrows down the facts to those that are the most fun and important. She suggests that young writers pick subjects that they know and like. That way they will enjoy writing a lot more.

Patricia and Fredrick McKissack

pages 58–71

This award-winning team wants to bring the past alive for young readers. Many of their books tell about African Americans who have made important contributions to the world. The McKissacks work well together. Fredrick McKissack does most of the research, while Patricia McKissack does most of the writing. Then, together, they rewrite until each book is just the way they want it.

"The people of the past have a great deal to teach us. We can learn from their tragedies and triumphs."

Jerry Pinkney *pages 10–23*

After he reads a manuscript for a book he is going to illustrate, Jerry Pinkney imagines what the characters look like. He does historical research about the subject, if he needs to. Pinkney also uses real people as models to help him develop the characters. He even keeps a closet full of interesting clothes for the models to wear. He lets them read the story and act it out! This way, Pinkney captures the right body movements and expressions for the characters in his drawings.

Books &

Author/Illustrator Study

More by Patricia and Fredrick McKissack

Carter G. Woodson: The Father of Black History
This biography tells the story of a man who wanted everyone to discover the achievements of African Americans.

Christmas in the Big House, Christmas in the Quarters
This book brings to life a holiday celebration from the past.

Flossie and the Fox
What happens when a little girl meets a fox in the woods? In her version of this old folk tale, Patricia McKissack creates two very memorable characters.

Fiction

Chang and the Paper Pony
by Eleanor Coerr
illustrated by Deborah Ray
In this story, set in the time of the California gold rush, a boy named Chang dreams of owning a pony of his own.

The Courage of Sarah Noble
by Alice Dalgliesh
Sarah is a pioneer and proud of it! She does what she can to help her family when they move west.

The Sunday Outing
by Gloria Pinkney
illustrated by Jerry Pinkney
Ernestine enjoys visiting with her great-grandmother in North Carolina and learning about all the things her parents and grandparents did long ago.

Nonfiction

Corn Is Maize
by Aliki
Did you know that people have been growing corn for thousands of years? This book tells how scientists have studied corn to learn about life in America long ago.

The Seminoles: A First American's Book
by Virginia Driving Hawk Sneve
illustrated by Ronald Himler
This book traces the history of the Seminole people and also tells how they live today.

xMedia

 Videos

 Software

Magazines

Videos

Follow The Drinking Gourd
Rabbit Ears
This animated tale tells how one brave family escaped from slavery. (30 minutes)

Paul Bunyan
SVS/Rabbit Ears
Meet a tall-tale hero from America's past! In this version of the classic story, the mighty logger ends up feeling sorry that he cut down so many trees—so he finds a way to make the forests green again. (30 minutes)

Software

20th Century Video Almanac Overview
Software Toolworks (IBM/CD-ROM)
This amazing reference source uses videos, photos, and sound to show you important events from the past hundred years.

Where in Time Is Carmen Sandiego?
Broderbund (Apple, Macintosh, IBM)
Carmen and her gang zoom through history in a time machine. Where are they headed? What are they planning? It's up to you to stop them!

Magazines

Children's Album
What items would you place in a time capsule to tell about life today? This magazine may help you think of ideas. It's full of artwork and writing by children as well as step-by-step instructions for lots of craft projects.

National Geographic World
This magazine allows you to travel around the world without leaving your chair. Read about archaeological discoveries, outdoor adventures, and more!

A Place to Write

Junior Philatelists of America
Post Office Box 1600
Trenton, NJ 08607

Stamps can tell you about a country's history. This club is for kids who are interested in stamp collecting. Write for information and the club newsletter. Include a self-addressed stamped envelope.

Acknowledgments

Grateful acknowledgment is made to the following sources for permission to reprint from previously published material. The publisher has made diligent efforts to trace the ownership of all copyrighted material in this volume and believes that all necessary permissions have been secured. If any errors or omissions have inadvertently been made, proper corrections will gladly be made in future editions.

Cover: Robert Tannenbaum.

Interior: "Home Place" from HOME PLACE by Crescent Dragonwagon, with illustrations by Jerry Pinkney. Text copyright © 1990 by Crescent Dragonwagon. Illustrations copyright © 1990 by Jerry Pinkney. This edition is reprinted by arrangement with Atheneum Books for Young Readers, Simon & Schuster Children's Publishing Division.

"Meet the Dirt Detectives" by Sheila Fairley reprinted with the permission of the publisher, OWL Magazine. OWL™ *The Discovery Magazine for Children* is published by The Young Naturalist Foundation. Logo used by permission. OWL and logo are trademarks of the Young Naturalist Foundation.

"Sunken Treasure" from SUNKEN TREASURE by Gail Gibbons. Copyright © 1988 by Gail Gibbons. Reprinted by permission of HarperCollins Publishers.

Photo of Armor of George Clifford, copyright ©1932 by The Metropolitan Museum of Art, New York (Munsey Fund, 1932, 32.130.6). "How to Create an Artifact Exhibit Card" text adaptation from INSIDE THE MUSEUM: A CHILDREN'S GUIDE TO THE METROPOLITAN MUSEUM OF ART by Joy Richardson. Published in 1993 by The Metropolitan Museum of Art, New York, and Harry N. Abrams, Incorporated, New York. Used by permission.

Selection and cover from PUEBLO STORYTELLER by Diane Hoyt-Goldsmith, illustrated by Lawrence Migdale. Text copyright © 1991 by Diane Hoyt-Goldsmith, photographs copyright © 1991 by Lawrence Migdale. Reprinted by permission of Holiday House, Inc.

Selection and cover from WILD AND WOOLLY MAMMOTHS by Aliki. Copyright © 1977 by Aliki Brandenberg. Reprinted by permission of HarperCollins Publishers.

"My Father's Grandfather and the Time Machine" by Staton Rabin. First published in *Cricket* Magazine. Copyright © 1991 by Staton Rabin. Reprinted by permission of the author. *Cricket* logo used by permission of Carus Publishing Company.

"The Fun They Had" by Isaac Asimov, adapted by Dwight Jon Zimmerman, illustrated by Evan Dorkin, from THE BANK STREET BOOK OF SCIENCE FICTION. Copyright © 1951 by NEA Service, Inc., copyright © 1989 by Byron Preiss Visual Publications, Inc. Cover illustration copyright © 1989 by Byron Preiss Visual Publications, Inc. Reprinted by permission.

"Kids Predict the Future" in *Scholastic News*, January 5, 1990. Copyright © 1990 by Scholastic Inc. Reprinted by permission.

Cover of FREDERICK DOUGLASS FIGHTS FOR FREEDOM by Margaret Davidson. Illustration copyright © 1968 by Scholastic Inc. Published by Scholastic Inc.

Cover of GEORGE WASHINGTON'S BREAKFAST by Jean Fritz, illustrated by Paul Galdone. Illustration copyright © 1969 by Paul Galdone. Published by Coward-McCann, Inc.

Cover from LET'S GO TRAVELING by Robin Rector Krupp. Illustrations copyright © 1992 by Robin Rector Krupp. Published by William Morrow & Company, Inc.

Cover of THREE NAMES by Patricia MacLachlan, illustrated by Alexander Pertzoff. Illustration copyright © 1991 by Alexander Pertzoff. Published by HarperCollins Publishers.

Photography and Illustration Credits

Photos: © John Lei for Scholastic Inc, all Tool Box items unless otherwise noted. p. 2 tl, cl: © Frank Cruz for Scholastic Inc.; shovel: © Richard Megna/Fundamental Photos for Scholastic Inc. pp. 2-3: © Frank Cruz for Scholastic Inc. p. 3 bc: © Frank Cruz for Scholastic Inc. p. 4 c: Ana Esperanza Nance for Scholastic Inc.; tc: © Telegraph Colour Library/FPG International Corp. p. 4 bl: Frank Cruz for Scholastic Inc. p. 5 c: Ana Esperanza Nance for Scholastic Inc.; tc: © FPG International Corp. p. 6 tc: © FPG International Corp.; c: © Ana Esperanza Nance for Scholastic Inc. p. 24-25: Nicholas Leibrecht; inset Courtesy of Mrs. George Williamson. p. 26: Nicholas Leibrecht. p. 27: Leif Peng. p. 28 cl: © Telegraph Colour Library/FPG International Corp.; all others: © Frank Cruz for Scholastic Inc. pp. 28-29: © Frank Cruz for Scholastic Inc. p. 29 c: © Frank Cruz for Scholastic Inc.; tr: © John Running; br: © David Waitz for Scholastic Inc. p. 30 all: © Frank Cruz for Scholastic Inc. p. 31 bl: © Keith Kent/Science Photo Library/Photo Researchers, Inc.; cr: © Frank Cruz for Scholastic Inc. p. 54 bl: © John Lei for Scholastic Inc.; bc: © Stanley Bach for Scholastic Inc. p. 55 br: © Frank Cruz for Scholastic Inc.; all others: © John Lei for Scholastic Inc. p. 58 br: © Deutshes Museum Munich. p. 59 cl: © Buffalo Bill Historical Center.; tr: © USC McKissick Columbia Photo; br: © All rights reserved McKissick Museum, The University of South Carolina. p. 60 cl: © Halley Ganges for Scholastic Inc.; br: © Ancient Art and Architecture Collection. p. 61 tl: © The Bettmann Archive; tr: © STB/Still Moving Picture Co.; br: © Scottish National Portrait Gallery. p. 62 tl, bc: © British Museum; tr: © Wyoming State Museum. p. 63 tl: © Museum of the City of New York; br: © American Philosophical Society. p. 64 tl: © Chris Luneski/Image Cascade; bl: © The Art Museum, Princeton University, Gift of the Arthur M. Sackler Foundation; cr: © Culver Pictures. p. 65 tl: © Smithsonian Institution, Washington D.C.; br: New York Times/Ana Esperanza Nance for Scholastic Inc. p. 66 tl, bl: © Stephen Trimble/Courtesy The Heard Museum; cr: © The Lincoln Museum, Fort Wayne, IN; br: © Lloyd Ostendorf Collection, Dayton ,OH. p. 67 cl, bl: © "Bird of Paradise" quilt top c.1860. Collection of the Museum of American Folk Art, New York; Gift of the trustees of the Museum of American Folk Art 1979.7.1 Bride's Quilt and detail; cr: © Art Resource, N.Y. p. 68 tl: © Portable Sundial, Silver and Gold, 10th Century (d). Canterbury Cathedral, Canterbury, Kent/Bridgeman Art Library, London; cr: National Museum of American History, book published by Harry N. Abrams Inc. p. 69 tl: © M. Renaudeau/ Agence Hoa-Qui; bl: © Lee Boltin/Boltin Picture Library; tr: © The Science Museum/Science and Society Picture Library. p. 70 bl: © Shelburne Museum; tr: © Margarete Busing/ Bildarchiv Preussischer Kalturbezitz. p. 71 cl, bl: © The Mexican Museum, San Francisco, CA., The Rockefeller Collection; tr: © Phil Johnson Ruth. p. 73 c: © Lawrence Migdale. p. 74 tl: © Lawrence Migdale. p. 75: © Jay Brousseau/The Image Bank. pp. 76-77: © Jay Brousseau/The Image Bank.̇ p. 77: © Jay Brousseau/The Image Bank. p. 78: © Jay Brousseau/The Image Bank. p. 79 bc: © Lawrence Migdale. pp. 80-81 c: Courtesy Denver Public Library, Western History Department. p. 82: framed picture: © John Lei for Scholastic Inc.; br: © Stanley Bach for Scholastic Inc. p. 83 br: © Frank Cruz for Scholastic Inc. pp. 86-95: © Letraset/Kirchoff/Wohlberg Inc. p. 113 c: © Superstock, Inc. pp. 114-115 c: © John Lei for Scholastic Inc. p. 116 bl: © John Lei for Scholastic Inc. p. 117 bl, cr: © Stanley Bach for Scholastic Inc.; bc, br: © John Lei for Scholastic Inc. p. 118 cl: © John Lei for Scholastic Inc.; br, bc: © Stanley Bach for Scholastic Inc. p. 119 cl, tr: © John Lei for Scholastic Inc.; br: © Frank Cruz for Scholastic Inc. p. 120 cr: © D. Cavagnero/Peter Arnold, Inc. p. 122 br: © George Lepp/Comstock. p. 123 bl: © Jane Grushow/Grant Heilman. p. 124 tl: Courtesy HarperCollins. p. 125 tr: Courtesy Holiday House. p. 127 br: © Stephen Ogilvy for Scholastic Inc.; bl: © John Gilmore/The Stock Market.

Illustrations: pp. 8-9, 56-57, 84-85: William Silvers; pp. 97-98, 100-102: Gail Piazza; pp. 104-112: Evan Dorkin.